This Texas cowboy of the early 1880s is proud of his birthplace, indicated by the stars stitched into the bottom brim of his hat. This photo was taken in Cheyenne, WY where the dapper cowhand undoubtedly purchased a new outfit after being paid off at the end of the drive. Jackson collection

These exciting images of cowboys at play were used for a colorful Wild West Show poster, circa 1910. These rough riders lived the fantasy life that young boys dream of imitating. The lithographed poster was printed around 1900 by the Donaldson Litho Co., Newport, KY.

No individual defined the image of the frontier more than William F. Cody, popularly known as Buffalo Bill. He was a Pony Express rider, Army scout, Indian fighter and buffalo hunter but his true fame came from his 30 years as a Wild West Show performer and entrepreneur.

In 1906 a small North Dakota flourmill commissioned young artist N. C. Wyeth to create a series of illustrations that would publicize their new breakfast cereal, Cream of Wheat. The title of this painting is "The Bronco Buster."

This pair of cowboys are showing off their new outfits, including their double action Colt revolvers. These are typical of well-heeled cowhands the 1880s and 90s. The saddle has angora saddle pockets on the back. Peck Collection

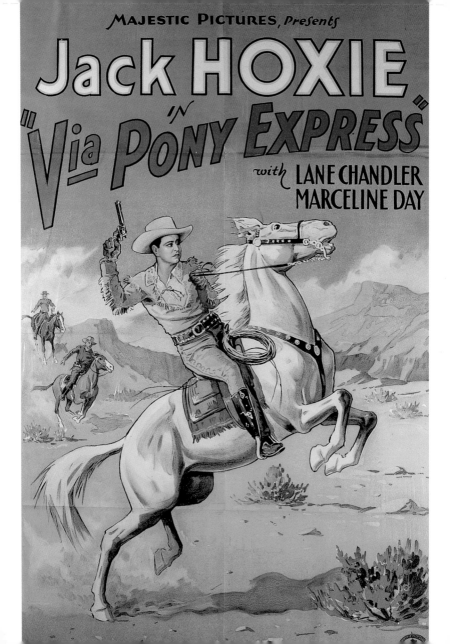

Jack Hoxie was a Wild West Show performer with the famous 101 Ranch until he made his first movie in 1913. This striking movie poster for *Via Pony Express* was made in 1934 by Majestic Pictures. Gish Collection

This well-heeled cowboy was prepared for anything man or nature could dish out. He was packing his Colt 6-Shooter, a Model 73 Winchester and was wearing spurs and chaps and bandanna. He even carried this toothbrush in the pocket of his vest, circa 1880. Peck Collection

THE NORMAN FILM MFG. CO.
PRESENTS

# BILL PICKETT
WORLD'S COLORED CHAMPION —in—

# 'THE BULL-DOGGER'

*Featuring The Colored Hero of the Mexican Bull Ring
in Death Defying Feats of Courage and Skill.*

## THRILLS! LAUGHS TOO!

Produced by NORMAN FILM MFG. CO.
JACKSONVILLE, FLA.

Bill Pickett achieved national notoriety for his bulldogging skill. This poster was for a silent movie titled *The Bull-Dogger*, made in 1923, featuring an all-black cast including Pickett. Bill was also a long time ranch hand and performer with the 101 Ranch in Oklahoma.

This little cowboy, circa 1890, was the son of parents who performed in a Wild West show. Children often learned roping and riding skills while watching their parents perform. Many later became performers themselves and some even went to Hollywood to become actors in western movies.

This illustration by R.G. Harris created in the 1920s for a pulp novel cover featured a hero blazing away with two six-guns. The carrying of two guns was virtually unheard of on the frontier but gorey pulp novels popularized this myth. Texas Ranger Museum collection.

Roy Rogers was known as "The King Of The
Cowboys." He was the nation's most popular
television star of the early 50's. He was a veteran of
over 100 feature western films beginning in 1938.
Along with his wife Dale Evans and horse Trigger
they starred in 100 TV episodes from 1951 to 57.

These shady-looking cowboys were characters in the title song "Four Bad Men From Arizona," from the Broadway play *The Cow-Boy Girl*, 1910. Cow-Boy Girl was an early name for cowgirls.

This dashing photograph was taken May 1, 1890. It is titled "Boys Headed For Dinner." The photo was taken on a ranch near Las Vegas, New Mexico.

# JOHN RUSKIN
## CIGAR

WAS 8¢

NOW 5¢

*Same Quality - Same Size*

The John Roscoe Cigar Co. used this image of a cowboy to promote the products. The carefree and reckless character of the cowboys typically guaranteed a successful sales campaign. This advertising poster would have been found hanging in a saloon in the early 1900s.

This Texas Ranger was a member of Company B. He posed with his horse in 1887. Along with his Colt revolver he carries a Bowie knife, as was typical for most Rangers and cowboys of the time. Jackson Collection

Silent movie star Tom Mix was one of Hollywood's most popular cowboy heroes. Mix had once been a hand on the famous 101 Ranch before moving on to Hollywood. He's pictured here in 1928 on a Henderson motorcycle.

This trio is decked out in new cowboy finery, including Colt 6-Shooters, Cheyenne-style holsters and shotguns chaps. They may be recently arrived easterners that decided to be photographed in their newly acquired outfits. Circa 1885. Peck collection

Frederick Remington was without a doubt the most
talented of the early western artists. He knew
cowboys and their way of life. This painting is titled
"Prospecting for Cattle Range." It features 2 well-
armed cattlemen searching for greener pastures.

In 1880 this group of Arizona cowboys posed for the camera. They are wearing outfits of typical working cowhands. Each is packing a "hog-leg" on their hip with cartridge belts full of .45s. Cowboys had to be prepared to abandon their duties and defend their lives during these dangerous days in the Arizona territory.

This wonderful embossed litho print illustration
depicts a cowboy of the 1890s. This illustration was
printed in Germany and was probably used in a
saloon as an advertisement for an alcoholic libation.
Manns Collection

A Wyoming cowboy of the 1880s. Wooly chaps made fron angora goat hide was very practical in the colder northern ranges. This cowboy has a rawhide quirt and rieta in his hands. By Cheyenne photographer C.D.Kirkland.

This illustration of a cowboy and his horse was one of many created for the J.B. Stetson hat company. The name Stetson was synonymous with cowboy hats. All cowboy hats were known as Stetsons even if that company didn't make them.

Many Indians took up ranching and became cowboys. This pair was decked out in typical outfits for 1910 cowhands, including white woolly chaps. An E. Smith photo.

# MILLER BROS. & ARLINGTON 101 RANCH REAL WILD WEST

## JOS. C. MILLER

THE REAL LEADER OF THE REAL WILD WEST. LEADING THE GRAND ENTREE OF OUR WORLD'S CHAMPION ROUGH RIDER.

This lithographed poster was produced for the 101 Ranch Real Wild West Show. The famous Miller Brothers took their Oklahoma show on the road off and on from 1905-16 and 1925-31 before finally going broke in the mid 1930s. They were one of the major Wild West Shows of the early 1900s.

This pair of dapper cowhands are fitted out in new outfits that include a pair of Colt six-shooters with cartridge/money belts. Peck Collection

# BUFFALO BILL'S
## WILD WEST

Buffalo Bill began his life as a Wild West show performer in 1886 and continued to travel and perform for the next 30 years. This poster was made in 1913 during the time he was performing with the Sells-Floto Circus. Manns Collection

William Boyd portrayed Hopalong Cassidy in a series of B westerns beginning in 1933. Hoppy, along with his popular horse Silver, made the transition into television with the series that ran from 1949 to 51.

This cowhand is reaching for his Winchester Model 1895 lever action rifle in order to dispatch the menacing grizzly coming up behind him. Winchester and every other gun maker used illustrations of cowboys and trappers in dangerous and breathtaking situations to help sell their weapons.

This Nebraska cowboy, circa 1905, poses proudly beside the saddle he undoubtedly won in a local rodeo. Bronc riders often wore woolly chaps during these times to help protect their legs when they hit the ground.

Exciting illustrations such as this one, produced in the 1930s, were used for one of the many pulp magazine covers. From about 1910 to the 1940s Western pulp novels were one of the most popular types of Western literature. The eye-catching covers depicted the daring exploits found within.